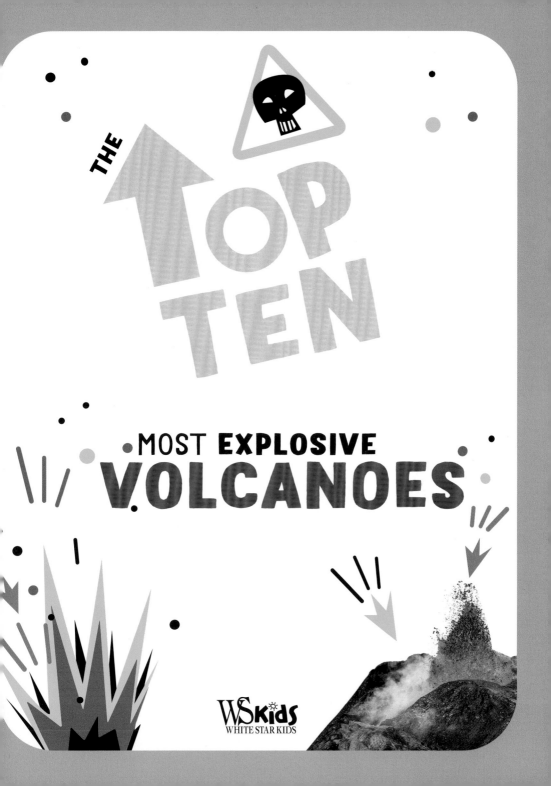

THE

TOP TEN

MOST EXPLOSIVE VOLCANOES

WSkids
WHITE STAR KIDS

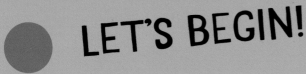

LET'S BEGIN!

THE RANKING OF THE TOP TEN MOST EXPLOSIVE VOLCANOES IS...UNPREDICTABLE!

Which volcano should be in first place?
The one that makes the loudest boom?
Or the one that shoots gas
and ash the farthest?
Are you sure?
Flip through the pages of this book to climb
the **Top Ten** and find out what volcanoes look like
and why and how they erupt.

EVEN IF YOU THINK YOU ALREADY KNOW EVERYTHING, KEEP READING. SURPRISES ARE JUST AROUND THE CORNER. DANGEROUS ONES!

LETHAL WEAPON

TRIVIA

Look for these symbols to learn unexpected
TRIVIA and discover what **LETHAL
WEAPONS** make these **TEN VOLCANOES**
worthy of our ranking!

THE DANGER LEVEL WILL INCREASE AS WE GO FROM **TEN**
ALL THE WAY UP TO TERRIBLE NUMBER **ONE**!

Hi, I'm **SAL**. Want to hear an awesome **LEGEND**? Well, people once said that salamanders like me can live amid flames, surrounded by lava. As cool as that sounds, nothing could be further from the truth. I'm trembling just thinking about it! But I'm very interested in volcanoes, so I've studied them extensively and **I'D LIKE TO COME ALONG AS YOU LEARN MORE ABOUT THEM**. Should we start with a little game?

Volcanoes are born when **MAGMA**, or glowing molten rock found **DEEP WITHIN EARTH**, escapes from an opening in Earth's crust. However, a lot of time can pass between **ERUPTIONS**. Based on their **ACTIVITY**, volcanoes are described in different ways.
FIND OUT BY FOLLOWING THE DOTTED LINES!

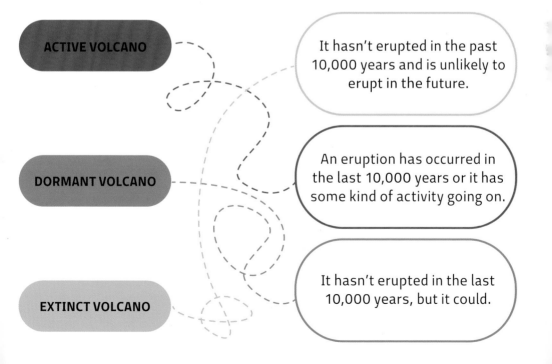

ACTIVE VOLCANO

DORMANT VOLCANO

EXTINCT VOLCANO

It hasn't erupted in the past 10,000 years and is unlikely to erupt in the future.

An eruption has occurred in the last 10,000 years or it has some kind of activity going on.

It hasn't erupted in the last 10,000 years, but it could.

THE WORLD'S LARGEST VOLCANO?

In this book, you'll find really explosive volcanoes, but...
YOU WON'T FIND THE WORLD'S LARGEST VOLCANO!
Do you know why? Because the Hawaiian giant known
as **MAUNA LOA**, like many other volcanoes similar to it,
isn't very hazardous at all.
This is because of the nature of the **LAVA** it produces.

In fact, the **LAVA** produced by Hawaiian volcanoes (unlike their more explosive "colleagues") is a free-flowing **LIQUID** and **NOT VERY VISCOUS**. As it exits the **CRATER**, it flows slowly and quietly down the slopes of the volcano, for stretches that can be quite long, like the water of a river.

In this way, all the **GASES** contained within it are dispersed in the air without causing **EXPLOSIONS** and damage.

TYPES OF VOLCANOES

If the word **"VOLCANO"** immediately makes you think of a smoking mountain, you're on the right track. But remember, that isn't always the case.
In fact, volcanoes can come in lots of different shapes and sizes. The main factors that determine the look and shape of a volcano are the **DURATION OF THE ERUPTION**, the **AMOUNT OF MATERIAL** that it releases, and the **TYPE OF LAVA THAT IS ERUPTED**, which, once cooled, turns into hard rock.

WE CAN DIVIDE VOLCANOES INTO CATEGORIES, ACCORDING TO CERTAIN SHARED FEATURES.
THE MAIN ONES ARE:

Shield

Many volcanoes spew out lava that is extremely hot (all lava is very hot, but this kind is even more so!) and very **FLUID**, which is why it flows for a few miles before cooling down. Because these volcanoes are wide and never too high, they resemble a **SHIELD** placed on the ground.

There are ancient shield volcanoes that are part of the Galapagos Islands. They range in age from 700,000 years to 4.2 million years old!

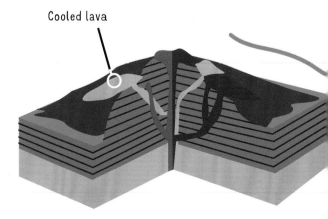

Cooled lava

Fissure vent

In these volcanoes, lava flows from a narrow **FISSURE** (a sort of opening) just a few feet wide, but that can reach several miles in length. A fissure is a **RIFT** that goes deep down into Earth's core.

Many underwater volcanoes are simple fissures and are located on large volcanic chains, such as the Mid-Atlantic Ridge, which spans the entire Atlantic from north to south.

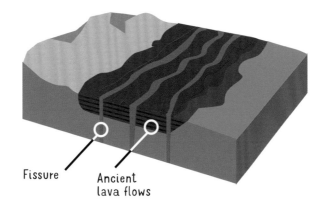

Fissure

Ancient lava flows

Cone or stratovolcano

Only **THE MOST EXPLOSIVE VOLCANOES** have this shape. To create it, **VISCOUS MAGMA** flows very slowly ("viscous" means it's sticky and thus doesn't flow easily), shaping a mountain with very steep slopes.
If violent eruptions alternate with calmer eruptions, a **STRATOVOLCANO**, composed of **OVERLAPPING LAYERS** of ash and solidified lava, is formed.

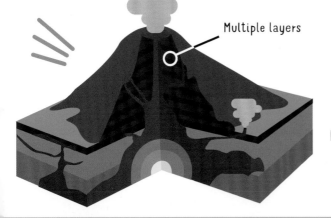

Multiple layers

In Indonesia, Kawah Ijen (Ijen crater) is composed of several stratovolcanoes, giving it a unique feature: It spouts out blue lava, colored by the large amount of sulfur it contains.

7

10 EYJAFJALLAJOKULL

ELEVATION: 5,466 ft
(1,666 m)

*Eyj... Ayja...
Eyjafjall...
I can't say it.
It's too hard!*

Can a volcano bring half a continent to a grinding halt? That's exactly what this Icelandic volcano did on April 15, 2010, when the immense **CLOUD OF ASH** produced by its eruption shut down airports and air traffic throughout much of Europe. But this volcano is dangerous in another way: Much of Eyjafjallajokull is covered by a **GLACIER** and, due to the sudden melting of its ice, an eruption could lead to catastrophic **FLOODS**!

TYPE:
Stratovolcano
(if you forgot what that means, reread the explanation on the previous page!)

LOCATION:
Iceland

LAST ACTIVE:
2010

LETHAL WEAPON

Jökulhlaup is an Icelandic word for an outburst flood caused by the melting of a glacier due to a volcanic eruption.

TRIVIA

The name of the volcano is really hard to pronounce. But its meaning in Icelandic is simple: "Glacier of the Island Mountains."

STRUCTURE OF A VOLCANO

Most classic volcanoes are similar to mountains, but they differ in that hot lava, gas, ash, molten rock fragments, and toxic fumes flow out of volcanoes. Each volcano consists of several parts that either make the eruption possible or are the product of it.

ALMOST ALL VOLCANOES SHARE THREE MAIN COMPONENTS.

Crater

Conduit (pipe)

Crater

At the top of a volcanic mountain is the crater, a basin shaped like a giant **BOWL**, which is formed during the **ERUPTION**. Way down at its base (which is often very deep) is the exit point where the **MAGMA** comes out. A volcano can have numerous other secondary side exits.

Craters endure even after the volcano stops erupting but are usually destroyed over time, either by other eruptions or by erosion.

Volcanic edifice

The body of the volcano, i.e., its **STRUCTURE**, is what looks like a mountain. It is usually shaped like a cone, but it can take on other forms as a result of **EXPLOSIONS** and the amount of lava that solidifies on its sides. Hidden inside is the **CONDUIT**, that is, the passage through which magma flows up from the deepest layers of Earth.

The highest volcanic edifice is found in the Andes. It belongs to the 22,569-foot-high (6,893 m) Ojos del Salado, but it's nothing compared to the Olympus Mons volcano on Mars, which is over 13.6 miles (25 km) high!

Magma chamber

Below the conduit, as if at the end of a corridor, is the **MAGMA CHAMBER**. That's where hot magma and gas are stored. The intense pressure generated inside can push the magma to seek an escape route, causing the volcano to erupt. An emptied magma chamber can cave in and form a **CALDERA**.

Volcanic edifice

Magma chamber

Lake Taupō occupies the caldera produced by one of the largest eruptions in history: that of a supervolcano in New Zealand 26,000 years ago.

COTOPAXI

ELEVATION:
19,347 ft
(5,897 m)

Cotopaxi is shaped like a **PERFECT CONE**, but don't be fooled by its beauty. This volcano is **DANGEROUS**! In the last three centuries, it has been active at least **50 TIMES**, with eruptions that have often had devastating effects on its surroundings due to flows of **BOILING MUDSLIDES** that descend at great speeds down the steep slopes of the mountain.

In 1877, that mud traveled 62 miles (100 km), only stopping before the Pacific Ocean and the mighty Amazon River.

TYPE:
Stratovolcano

LOCATION:
Ecuador

LAST ACTIVE:
2016

LETHAL WEAPON
Boiling mud.

TRIVIA
It's shaped like
a perfect cone!

13

NYIRAGONGO

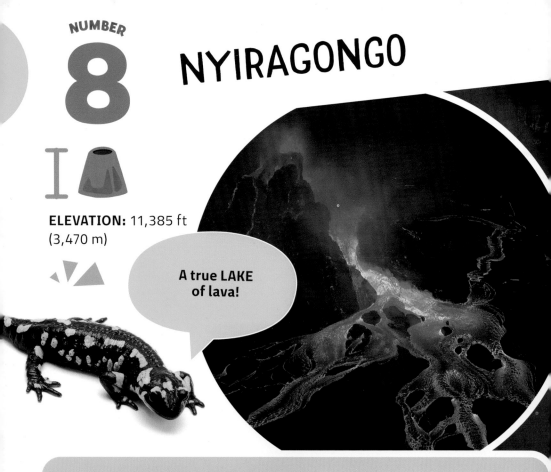

ELEVATION: 11,385 ft
(3,470 m)

A true LAKE
of lava!

Set in the East African Rift Valley, the region where the first **HOMINIDS** developed, Nyiragongo has a lava lake within its **CRATER** that is 0.75 miles wide (1.2 km) at its rim, and more than 656 feet (200 m) deep, making it the largest in the world.

This lava lake slowly fills with magma, and when it overflows, rivers of **VERY FLUID LAVA** flow quickly down the sides of the volcano. They can reach speeds of 62 MPH (100 kph) and cover the entire area around them.

TYPE:
Stratovolcano

LOCATION:
Democratic Republic of the Congo

LAST ACTIVE:
2022

LETHAL WEAPON

Its gas! Why? To find out more, you'll have to take the explosive quiz at the end of the book!

TRIVIA

It's considered one of the most active volcanoes in the world.

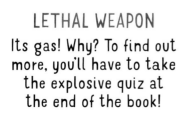

MOUNT SAINT HELENS

ELEVATION: 8,363 ft
(2,549 m)

BOOOOM!

May 18, 1980, was a memorable day for volcanologists.

After 123 years of total inactivity, the Saint Helens volcano showed everyone how **DEVASTATINGLY POWERFUL** it is with an eruption that destroyed an entire centuries-old forest and killed thousands of animals in just **3 MINUTES**.

Currently, a **BUILDUP OF LAVA** is forming again within the volcano, and scientists worry that it might give rise to another **EXTREMELY EXPLOSIVE ERUPTION**.

TYPE:
Stratovolcano

LOCATION:
United States

LAST ACTIVE:
2008

LETHAL WEAPON
A huge landslide
of debris.

TRIVIA
Its 1980 eruption was the most
catastrophic volcanic event in the
history of the United States of America.

EXPLOSIVE ERUPTIONS!

Each volcano is different due to the nature of the lava that erupts, the pressure it's subjected to, and the amount of **GAS** and **BURNING ASH AND DUST** that are emitted. Thus, danger levels can vary even among the most **EXPLOSIVE** volcanoes. For that reason, scientists have created categories based on the **VOLCANIC EXPLOSIVITY INDEX**.

IN ASCENDING ORDER, THE MOST EXPLOSIVE TYPES OF ERUPTIONS ARE:

Strombolian

Strombolian eruptions are moderately **EXPLOSIVE**. Incandescent lava is intermittently spouted from a crater on the summit of the volcano, and its **SPATTER** creates a sort of light show, visible especially at night. These eruptions produce many **LAPILLI** (small stony fragments of lava) the size of walnuts.

The Italian volcano Stromboli, in the Aeolian Islands, is constantly erupting with small hourly explosions that send lapilli soaring.

Vulcanian

This type of eruption emits **DENSE, THICK MAGMA**, often accompanied by really loud, intense explosions. With the magma, large amounts of **ASH-LADEN GAS** are shot upwards, forming mushroom clouds. **VOLCANIC BOMBS**, that is, pieces of glowing rock at least the size of a human hand, are spewed out from the main vent.

Vulcan was the name of the Roman god of fire, who happened to also be a very skilled blacksmith. According to legend, he shaped Jupiter's thunderbolts in a workshop located inside a volcano.

Peléan and Plinian

These are the deadliest, most **DESTRUCTIVE** kinds of eruptions and can last for many days. They produce large quantities of **ASH** and **GAS** that can be carried on the wind for miles. Sometimes an **AVALANCHE** of glowing volcanic ash speeds down the mountainside with the force of a hurricane, instantly burning everything in its path.

Peléan eruptions are named after the Pelée volcano in Martinique. Curiously and coincidentally, Pele is also the name of the powerful Hawaiian goddess of fire who is said to dwell inside a volcano.

VOLCANIC ROCKS

Volcanic rocks are formed when **LAVA COOLS** as it flows above Earth's surface.

THE SPEED AT WHICH THE LAVA COOLS DETERMINES THE APPEARANCE AND CONSISTENCY OF THE RESULTING ROCK.
HERE ARE THREE VERY DIFFERENT EXAMPLES.

Basaltic rocks

Basalt is the most **COMMON** volcanic rock on Earth. In fact, it makes up much of the **OCEAN FLOOR**. It is very dark in color, a sort of gray, and it is formed by mineral crystals so small that they're very hard to see. Cooling rapidly, those crystals didn't have enough **TIME** to grow. If you want to get a good look at basalt, get a magnifying glass!

Sometimes, because of rapid cooling, fractures are created in the lava, forming true basalt columns.

Obsidian

When **LAVA** cools very quickly, almost instantaneously, no crystals can form at all. The rock that is generated looks very much like **GLASS**, and its edges are equally sharp. This volcanic glass, called **OBSIDIAN**, is usually **BLACK**. It often forms where lava comes into contact with water or if it cooled as it flew through the air.

Obsidian fragments have sharp edges and were used in ancient times to make knives, arrowheads, spearheads, various cutting tools, and ornamental objects.

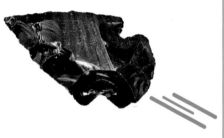

Pumice

Pumice is formed during **EXPLOSIVE** eruptions and, like obsidian, is considered a type of **GLASS**. It is usually light in color and can range in size from tiny dust particles to boulders the size of a house. It looks a lot like a **SPONGE** because of the many small pores left by the **GASES** that were trapped in the lava before it cooled down.

The empty spaces make the rock lighter, and, if you put pumice in water, they act as little life preservers that keep the stone afloat!

6

VESUVIUS

ELEVATION: 4,203 ft (1,281 m)

It's a double volcano. What does that mean? Find out below!

Here's the most **FAMOUS VOLCANO IN THE WORLD**: Mount Vesuvius.

It's a **DOUBLE VOLCANO** because it was formed within an older volcanic structure, Mount Somma, soon becoming taller than its predecessor. It's the only active volcano in Europe that is not on an island.

Its eruptions have always been **EXPLOSIVE**, with rapidly moving magma and flows of incandescent **GASES**.

TYPE:
Stratovolcano

LOCATION:
Italy

LAST ACTIVE:
1944

LETHAL WEAPON

Vesuvius is considered one of the most dangerous volcanoes in the world because of its proximity to the city of Naples and the many towns built on its slopes.

TRIVIA

It's famous around the world for one eruption in particular: Find out which one by turning the page!

HISTORIC ERUPTIONS!

Throughout history, devastating eruptions in various parts of the world have left very obvious marks, both in the stories handed down from generation to generation and in the transformation of the land.

HERE ARE TWO ERUPTIONS THAT ARE UNFORGETTABLE FOR THEIR TERRIBLE IMPACT!

Pompeii

A volcanic event of great historical importance occurred in the Roman city of **POMPEII**, Italy, in 7<u>9</u> CE. We know what happened because it was described in detail by **PLINY THE YOUNGER**. Vesuvius erupted and the city was **COMPLETELY BURIED** under a thick layer of **ASH** and **PUMICE**. Ironically, that debris has preserved the city up to the present day.

Tambora

Abundant dust in the atmosphere blocked the light of the sun, precipitation increased, and Earth's surface cooled a little everywhere so that summer never came that year.

Although more than **200 YEARS** have passed, memory remains of the eruption of this Indonesian volcano, which, in April 1815, killed about **10,000 PEOPLE**. The intensity of the eruption pushed a jet of ash and gas more than 25 miles (40 km) into the air, causing changes to the weather and climate that had devastating effects all over the world!

AIRA CALDERA (SAKURAJIM

ELEVATION:
3,665 ft
(1,117 m)

Twenty-two thousand years ago, a powerful **EXPLOSION** created the Aira caldera, which has a diameter of 12 miles (20 km) and houses **SAKU-RAJIMA** within it. At 15,000 years old, it's Japan's most active volcano. Today, Sakurajima continuously releases large amounts of **ASH**, which fall to the ground depending on the way the wind is blowing, covering everything, including people. That ash, however, makes the soil very **FERTILE**.

TYPE:
Caldera

LOCATION:
Japan

LAST ACTIVE:
2022

26

LETHAL WEAPON

Eruptions that are very short, but intense and frequent.

TRIVIA

The largest radishes in the world are grown on its slopes!

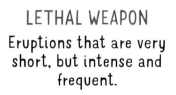

POPOCATÉPETL

ELEVATION: 17,802 ft (5,426 m)

This volcano is erupting right now!

"Smoking mountain" is the meaning of this volcano's **AZTEC** name. And it lives up to its reputation, called **EL POPO** by locals. In addition to its considerable height, El Popo has a giant crater that's more than 2,000 feet (600 m) wide, with **VERY STEEP** walls. Over the course of its **730,000 YEARS** it has had numerous catastrophic eruptions, evidenced by the rocks found in the area. Since the last eruption in 2004, **WHICH IS STILL ONGO-ING**, smoke is constantly coming out of the crater, rising up 0.2 to 1.25 miles (1-2 km) above the mountain.

TYPE:
Stratovolcano

LOCATION:
Mexico

LAST ACTIVE:
2022

LETHAL WEAPON

It keeps everyone on their toes because of its continuous activity.

TRIVIA

In Aztec mythology, Popocatépetl was a warrior transformed into a volcano by the gods.

3

PINATUBO

ELEVATION: 4,875 ft
(1,486 m)

This volcano sure got up on the wrong side of the bed! Find out why below!

The existence of this volcano became well known throughout the world only after its **VIOLENT ERUPTION** on June 15, 1991, one of the **LARGEST** in the 20th century.

Huge quantities of **GAS** and **ASH** soon covered an area of more than 38,000 square miles (100,000 km²).

There was so much **DUST** that it changed the **TEMPERATURE OF THE PLANET**, cooling Earth's surface by about half a degree on average for more than two years.

TYPE:
Stratovolcano

LOCATION:
The Philippines

LAST ACTIVE:
2021

LETHAL WEAPON
The amount of dust that
it was able to launch.

TRIVIA
Before the great eruption,
the volcano had been "asleep"
for 600 years.

2

SANTA MARIA

ELEVATION:
12,375 ft
(3,772 m)

> Here we are at the second most explosive volcano! But which one will come in at #1?

The awakening of the Santa Maria volcano in the fall of 1902 came after more than **500 YEARS OF INACTIVITY**, pre-announcing its arrival a few months earlier by a series of strong **EARTHQUAKES**.
The eruption, ranked among the most **INTENSE** of the past 200 years, resulted in abundant flows of **LAVA** and a **RIFT** on the side of the volcano, destroying much of the **CONE** with its powerful explosions.

TYPE:
Stratovolcano

LOCATION:
Guatemala

LAST ACTIVE:
2022

LETHAL WEAPON

Very high destructive capacity, based on the effects of the 1902 eruption.

TRIVIA

The volcanic ash emitted on that occasion was found more than 2,500 miles (4,000 km) away.

KRAKATOA

ELEVATION: 2,667 ft (813 m)

It's always the smallest ones that are the most dangerous!

Krakatoa is number one on our Top Ten list because it's considered to be **THE MOST DANGEROUS VOLCANO EVER!** It has been "reborn" within the caldera, partially **BELOW THE SEA**, which had formed after a frightening eruption in late August 1883. The explosion was so powerful that it caused the destruction of most of the archipelago where the volcano was located. It is said that the **BOOM** of its eruption was heard almost 3,100 miles (5,000 km) away!

TYPE:
Caldera

LOCATION:
Indonesia

LAST ACTIVE:
2022

LETHAL WEAPON

A boom so loud that it
damaged the eardrums of
people within a radius of
40 miles (64 km)
from the volcano.

TRIVIA

The ash cloud it created was so
thick that it obscured the sun
over Indonesia for several days.

EXPLOSIVE QUESTIONS

TRY ANSWERING THESE QUESTIONS, BUT DON'T BE AFRAID TO GET THEM WRONG! TURN THE PAGE FOR THE CORRECT ANSWERS.

10- HOW DID THE LAST ERUPTION OF EYJAFJALLAJOKULL IMPACT THE LOCAL INHABITANTS?

A It burned their houses

B It damaged local crops

C It made the air unbreathable

9- WHICH RARE ANIMAL SPECIES LIVES ON COTOPAXI?

A A hummingbird

B A butterfly

C A frog

8- BESIDES RIVERS OF MAGMA, WHAT MAKES NYIRAGONGO SO LETHAL?

A Glowing ash

B Falling boulders

C Toxic gases

7- WHAT DID MOUNT SAINT HELENS LOOK LIKE BEFORE THE 1980 ERUPTION?

A Lower than today

B Higher than today

C Same height as today

6- WHAT MAKES THE VOLCANOLOGY OBSERVATORY CREATED TO MONITOR VESUVIUS SO UNIQUE?

A It's the world's oldest observatory

B It's the world's highest altitude observatory

C It's the world's smallest observatory

5- WHAT HAPPENED AFTER THE AIRA CALDERA ERUPTED IN 1914?

A A peninsula was formed

B A rare species of bird went extinct

C The fallen ash formed a mountain

4- WHAT IS LOCATED AT THE BASE OF THE POPOCATÉPETL VOLCANO?

A Saltwater lakes

B Caves and underground tunnels

C Ancient monasteries

3- WHAT DID PINATUBO LOOK LIKE BEFORE THE 1991 ERUPTION?

A It had a high, pointed peak

B It was round and home to a forest

C It was a valley crossed by a river

2- WHAT KIND OF CROPS ARE GROWN AT THE FOOT OF THE SANTA MARIA VOLCANO?

A Corn

B Coffee

C Rice

1- WHAT OTHER DISASTROUS PHENOMENON DID THE 1883 ERUPTION OF KRAKATOA CAUSE?

A A flood

B A fire

C A tsunami

EXPLOSIVE
ANSWERS

10, B The eruption had a major impact on agriculture in Iceland. Poisonous gases produced during the eruption polluted the soil and contaminated the water, causing widespread damage to livestock farming as well.

9, A On the slopes of Cotopaxi, a rare high-altitude hummingbird, *Oreotrochilus chimborazo*, just 5 inches (12 cm) long, has been discovered nesting at more than 13,000 feet (4,000 m) above sea level.

8, C Carbon dioxide, called *mazuku* by the locals, comes out of the volcano's soil and is deadly if not quickly dispersed by the wind.

7, B Before it erupted, Mount Saint Helens was 9,675 feet (2,949 m) high. As a result of that powerful explosion, the largest landslide in history was created on the summit, causing the mountain to drop 1,312 feet (400 m) in height.

6, A Built at the behest of Ferdinand II of the Two Sicilies (House of Bourbon), the Vesuvius Observatory has been in operation since 1841 and was the very first of its kind. The earliest volcanological and seismic research in the world was conducted here.

5, A The 1914 eruption was so powerful that the island on which the volcano was located incorporated several small islands nearby and turned into a peninsula, connecting to the mainland.

4, A On the slopes of Popocatépetl there are numerous monasteries built by different orders of friars in the early 16th century, now part of a World Heritage Site.

3, B Before 1991, Pinatubo consisted of a set of small, highly eroded, forest-covered highlands. After it erupted, a small caldera formed on the summit, the bottom of which is now covered by a lake.

2, B Despite the imminent danger, many people live on the slopes of the Santa Maria volcano, cultivating its fertile soil, which is particularly suitable for growing a highly prized kind of coffee.

1, C The collapse of the volcanic edifice caused so much rock to fall into the sea that it created tsunami waves 130 feet (40 m) high.

CRISTINA BANFI

With a degree in natural sciences from the University of Milan, Cristina Banfi has taught at several schools. She has been involved in science communication and education for more than 20 years and has been part of publishing projects in both scholastic and popular fields, particularly for children and young people. In recent years, she has written several books for White Star.

PHOTO CREDITS

All photographs are from Shutterstock except the following:
Getty Images pages 16 right, 19 top, 21 bottom, 30–31, 32–33;
White Star page 24; NASA page 25.

Editorial Coordination
Giada Francia

Graphic design and layout
Valentina Figus

WSKids
WHITE STAR KIDS

White Star Kids™ is a trademark of White Star s.r.l.

© 2023 White Star s.r.l.
Piazzale Luigi Cadorna, 6
20123 Milan, Italy
www.whitestar.it

Translation: Katherine Kirby
Editing: Michele Suchomel-Casey

ISBN 978-88-544-1992-6
 2 3 4 5 6 27 26 25 24 23

Printed and manufactured in China by
Dream Colour (Hong Kong) Printing Limited

FSC
www.fsc.org
MIX
Paper from
responsible sources
FSC® C178000